THE HEALING PATH: UNDERSTANDING PSYCHOLOGICAL EFFECTS OF LOSS AND MOURNING

DAVID PEDRO

aa**The Healing Path: Understanding Psychological Effects of Loss and Mourning**

Chapter 1: The Journey of Grief

- Understanding Grief: A Natural Response

- The Different Faces of Mourning

- The Importance of Acknowledging Loss

Chapter 2: Spiritual Healing Through Loss

- The Role of Spirituality in Grief

- Healing Practices for the Grieving Soul

- Finding Strength in Faith and Belief

Chapter 3: Mediumship and Spirit Communication

- Exploring Mediumship: Connecting with the Beyond

- Signs from Loved Ones: Recognising Messages

- The Therapeutic Benefits of Spirit Communication

Chapter 4: Cultural Perspectives on the Afterlife

- Understanding Diverse Beliefs About Death

- How Culture Shapes Our Grieving Process

- Lessons from Global Traditions in Mourning

Chapter 5: Rituals and Ceremonies for Honouring the Departed

- The Power of Ritual in Healing

- Creating Personal Ceremonies of Remembrance

- Community Practices and Their Impact.

The Healing Path: Understanding Psychological Effects of Loss and Mourning

The journey of grief is a deeply personal and multifaceted experience, one that unfolds in layers and invites us to confront the complexities of loss. Understanding the psychological effects of loss and mourning is crucial for anyone navigating this path. Grieving is not merely an emotional response; it encompasses a range of psychological reactions that can affect our mental, emotional, and even spiritual well-being. Acknowledging these effects can empower us to move forward with intention, fostering both healing and connection to our departed loved ones.

In the face of loss, individuals often experience a whirlwind of emotions, ranging from profound sadness to anger, confusion, and even guilt. Each emotion serves a purpose in the grieving process, offering a way to reflect on the relationship shared with the deceased. It is important to give ourselves permission to feel and process these emotions without judgment. By doing so, we create space for healing, allowing ourselves to honour the memories and love that remain. Understanding that this emotional spectrum is a natural response to loss can help us cultivate compassion for ourselves during this difficult time.

The psychological effects of mourning extend beyond immediate emotional responses; they can also manifest in changes to our daily lives, relationships, and self-identity. As we grapple with the absence of a loved one, we may find ourselves questioning our place in the world or feeling disconnected from those around us. This sense of isolation is common and can be mitigated by seeking support from others who understand our journey. Engaging in grief counselling or connecting with spiritual healers can provide valuable insights and tools to navigate the complexities of mourning, fostering resilience and hope for the future.

Cultural perspectives on grief and loss offer profound insights that can enrich our understanding of the mourning process. Different cultures have unique rituals and ceremonies that honour the departed, serving as a reminder of the interconnectedness of life and death. These practices can provide comfort, allowing individuals to express their grief in meaningful ways. By exploring these diverse approaches, we can learn from the wisdom of others, integrating elements that resonate with our personal beliefs and experiences. This cultural exploration not only honours the memory of our loved ones but also reinforces our own healing journey.

Finally, the role of dreams and the spiritual connection to those we have lost can be a source of solace and inspiration. Many people report vivid dreams or signs from their departed loved ones, which can offer reassurance during the grieving process. Recognizing these experiences as valid and meaningful can help us maintain a sense of connection beyond the physical realm. Reflecting on philosophical notions of life after death further encourages us to consider the continuity of love and relationships, fostering a hopeful outlook. By embracing these perspectives, we not only honour our grief but also celebrate the enduring spirit of those we have lost.

Chapter 1: The Journey of Grief

Understanding Grief: A Natural Response

Grief is a profound and intricate emotion that touches everyone at some point in their lives. It is a natural response to loss, showing the depth of love and connection we share with those who have passed on. Understanding grief as a natural process can be empowering, allowing us to navigate our feelings with greater compassion and insight. In the journey of mourning, acknowledging grief as a universal experience helps us to embrace our own emotions while also understanding the experiences of others. This chapter aims to illuminate the transformative power of grief and how it can serve as a pathway to healing.

When we lose someone dear to us, the initial shock can feel overwhelming. It is essential to recognise that this emotional turmoil is a natural reaction to the severing of a bond that held significant meaning. Grief encompasses a spectrum of feelings, from sadness and anger to confusion and even relief. Each person experiences grief differently, influenced by their unique relationship with the departed. In this context, it is vital to honour our individual journeys while also acknowledging the shared human experience of loss. By embracing our emotions without judgment, we can begin to understand the lessons grief teaches us about love, resilience, and the fragility of life.

Cultural perspectives on mourning and the afterlife offer valuable insights into the diverse ways people cope with loss. Many cultures incorporate rituals and ceremonies that honour the departed, providing comfort and a sense of community during challenging times. These practices not only help individuals process their grief but also serve to reinforce connections with the spiritual realm. Engaging in such rituals can foster a sense of belonging and continuity, reminding us that love transcends physical existence. By exploring these cultural traditions, we can find inspiration to create our own meaningful practices that resonate with our beliefs and values.

The psychological effects of loss can be profound, often leading to feelings of isolation or despair. However, acknowledging these emotions is a crucial step toward healing. It is essential to seek support, whether through grief counselling or connecting with others who share similar experiences. Sharing our stories in a safe environment can validate our feelings and help us nd solace in the knowledge that we are not alone. Additionally, exploring the role of dreams in connecting with loved ones can provide comfort and insight, as many individuals report receiving messages or guidance from those who have passed. Embracing these experiences can deepen our understanding of the bonds we share, even beyond the physical realm.

Ultimately, grief is not just a sign of loss but also a testament to the love we have experienced. It invites us to think on the meaning of life, the nature of relationships, and our beliefs about the afterlife. Engaging with philosophical reflections on life after death can help us cultivate a sense of peace and acceptance as we navigate our feelings. As we walk the healing path, let us remember that grief is a natural response that honours our connections, fosters resilience, and ultimately leads us toward greater understanding and spiritual growth. Embracing this journey can transform our sorrow into a celebration of love, allowing us to carry the essence of our departed loved ones within us as we continue to live and heal.

The Different Faces of Mourning

Mourning is a deeply personal and multifaceted experience that manifests in many ways, shaped by individual personalities, cultural backgrounds, and spiritual beliefs. Understanding these different faces of mourning can provide valuable insights for those navigating their own grief or supporting others through the process. It is essential to recognize that mourning is not a linear journey; rather, it encompasses a range of emotions and expressions that can vary dramatically from one person to another. This chapter seeks to explore the diverse dimensions of mourning, offering hope and encouragement to those during their healing journey.

One of the most profound aspects of mourning is the emotional spectrum it encompasses. While sadness is often the most recognized expression of grief, other emotions such as anger, guilt, and confusion frequently accompany it. For some, mourning may manifest through an overwhelming sense of longing for the departed, while others might find solace in moments of joy as they recall cherished memories. This emotional complexity can be confusing, but it is important to remember that such feelings are a natural part of the healing process. Embracing these emotions without judgment can pave the way for deeper understanding and eventual acceptance.

Cultural perspectives play a significant role in shaping how individuals experience and express mourning. Different cultures have distinct rituals and practices that honour the deceased, providing frameworks for grief that can be both comforting and enlightening. These rituals often serve as communal touchstones, creating a shared space for individuals to express their sorrow and celebrate the lives of those they have lost. By exploring and incorporating various cultural mourning practices, individuals can find new ways to connect with their grief, allowing for a richer and more holistic healing experience.

Spiritual beliefs also profoundly influence the mourning journey. For many, the connection to the afterlife and the possibility of ongoing communication with departed loved ones can provide immense comfort. Mediumship and spirit communication offer a pathway for individuals to seek reassurance and closure, allowing them to feel the presence of their loved ones even after death. Engaging in practices such as meditation, prayer, or attending spiritual gatherings can foster a sense of connection that transcends the physical realm, reminding mourners that love endures beyond death.

Lastly, the role of dreams in the grieving process cannot be understated. Many individuals report vivid dreams where they encounter their loved ones, often feeling a sense of peace and closure upon awakening. These dreams can serve as powerful reminders of the ongoing bond shared with the departed, offering solace and guidance during difficult times. By reflecting on these experiences, individuals can cultivate a deeper understanding of their grief and its transformative potential. Philosophical reflections on life after death can also inspire hope, encouraging mourners to consider the possibility of love continuing beyond the physical existence. As we navigate the different faces of mourning, it is crucial to honour our unique emotional landscapes while remaining open to the myriad possibilities for healing and connection.

The Importance of Acknowledging Loss

The journey through loss is one of the most profound experiences that we face in life and acknowledging that loss is a crucial step in the healing process. When we allow ourselves to fully recognize and accept our grief, we create space for healing and transformation. This acknowledgment is not merely an act of remembrance; it is a powerful declaration of love for those we have lost. It reinforces our connection to them, reminding us that their presence continues to resonate in our lives, even in their absence. By embracing our feelings of loss, we honour their memory and affirm the significance of our shared experiences.

In the context of spiritual healing and grief counselling, recognizing loss fosters an environment where healing can occur. This process invites us to explore our emotions deeply, allowing us to confront the pain rather than sidestep it. By doing so, we can better understand the psychological effects of mourning, which often manifest as sadness, anger, or confusion. Acknowledging these emotions paves the way for constructive conversations with grief counsellors or spiritual healers, who can guide us through the complexities of our grief. Such dialogues can be profoundly therapeutic, helping us to articulate our feelings and find solace in shared experiences.

Cultural perspectives on the afterlife further illuminate the importance of recognizing loss. Many cultures have intricate rituals and ceremonies that honour the departed, serving as communal acknowledgments of grief. These practices not only validate individual feelings of loss but also reinforce the belief that our loved ones continue to exist in some form beyond physical death. Engaging in such rituals can provide comfort, creating a sense of connection to those who have passed away. This collective acknowledgment of loss fosters healing within communities, reminding us that we are not alone in our grief.

Dreams also play an essential role in our process of acknowledging loss. Many people report vivid dreams of their departed loved ones, often feeling a sense of comfort and connection during these encounters. These dreams can serve as a bridge between the physical and spiritual realms, offering insights and messages that validate our feelings of loss. By recognizing these dreams as meaningful experiences, we can find solace in the idea that our loved ones are still with us in some way, guiding us and providing reassurance during our healing journey.

Finally, reflecting philosophically on life after death can enrich our understanding of loss. Engaging with these ideas encourages us to contemplate the nature of existence and what it means to love and lose. This exploration can lead to profound insights about life, love, and the enduring connections we share with those who have passed. By acknowledging our loss, we not only honour the memories of our loved ones but also open ourselves up to the possibility of continued connection and growth. Embracing this journey of acknowledgment is not just about mourning; it is about celebrating the love that transcends even the boundaries of death.

Chapter 2: Spiritual Healing Through Loss

The Role of Spirituality in Grief

In the journey of grief, spirituality serves as a vital companion, offering solace and understanding during one of life's most challenging experiences. For many, the pain of loss can feel isolating, leading to a profound sense of disconnection not only from the departed but also from oneself. Engaging with spirituality invites individuals to explore deeper dimensions of existence, fostering a connection that transcends the physical realm. This exploration can manifest in various forms, from personal reflections to community rituals, all of which can help to illuminate the path toward healing.

The Healing Path: Understanding Psychological Effects of Loss and Mourning

Spirituality provides a framework for understanding the complexities of loss, allowing individuals to find meaning in their grief. For some, this might involve the belief in an afterlife or the continued presence of loved ones in spirit. Such beliefs can transform mourning from a solely painful experience into a journey of love and remembrance. By embracing spiritual perspectives, grieving individuals can discover that their relationship with the departed is not con ned to memories but can evolve into a dynamic connection that continues to influence their lives. This shift in perception can be a powerful source of comfort, helping to mitigate feelings of despair.

Furthermore, the role of rituals and ceremonies in the grieving process cannot be overstated. Many cultures have long embraced the practice of honouring the dead through spiritual rituals, which serve to acknowledge the loss while simultaneously celebrating the life that was lived. These ceremonies—whether they are grand communal gatherings or intimate personal moments—create sacred spaces where loved ones can process their emotions and share their experiences. Engaging in such practices can provide a sense of continuity, reinforcing the belief that love endures beyond physical separation. This communal aspect of spirituality fosters connection, reminding individuals that they are not alone in their grief.

The influence of dreams in connecting with departed loved ones also highlights the profound interplay between spirituality and grief. Many people report experiencing vivid dreams that provide messages or comfort from those who have passed away. These dreams can serve as powerful reminders of the bond that remains, encouraging mourners to remain open to the signs and communication from the spirit world. Such experiences can validate the feelings of loss while simultaneously offering hope and reassurance, prompting individuals to reflect on the nature of existence and the ongoing journey of the soul.

Ultimately, integrating spirituality into the grieving process encourages a holistic approach to healing. It invites individuals to honour their emotions while also exploring the broader questions of life, death, and what lies beyond. Embracing these spiritual dimensions allows for a deeper understanding of loss, fostering resilience and hope amidst the pain. By acknowledging the role of spirituality in grief, loved ones can find not only healing but also a renewed sense of purpose, ensuring that the legacy of their departed continues to inspire and illuminate their path forward.

Healing Practices for the Grieving Soul

Healing from loss is a journey that often feels overwhelming, but engaging in healing practices can provide solace and guidance for the grieving soul. These practices, rooted in various traditions and philosophies, serve as bridges to understanding the depths of our emotions and the connections we maintain with those who have passed. By embracing spiritual healing methods, individuals can find comfort and a renewed sense of purpose amidst their sorrow, allowing them to navigate their grief in a manner that honours both their pain and their loved one's memory.

One effective approach to healing is the incorporation of rituals and ceremonies designed to honour the departed. These acts serve not only as commemorations but also as powerful expressions of love and remembrance. Whether it's lighting candles, creating memory altars, or participating in community gatherings, rituals can foster a sense of connection and closure. Engaging in such practices enables individuals to articulate their grief in a sacred space, allowing them to feel supported by both the physical and spiritual realms. These moments can be transformative, turning sorrow into a celebration of life and legacy.

Mediumship and spirit communication also play a significant role in the healing process. Many find comfort in connecting with a medium who can facilitate communication with the departed, offering messages of love and reassurance. These connections can serve as reminders that love transcends physical existence, providing a sense of continuity that can be profoundly healing. By embracing these experiences, individuals may find that their grief is softened, allowing for moments of joy amidst the sadness as they feel the presence of their loved ones guiding them through the journey of mourning.

Cultural perspectives on the afterlife further enrich the healing experience, as they provide diverse frameworks for understanding loss. Many traditions emphasize the importance of community and shared mourning, reminding us that we are not alone in our grief. Exploring these cultural practices can offer new insights and methods of coping, inspiring individuals to adopt rituals that resonate with their beliefs and emotional needs. This exploration can also foster a greater appreciation for the interconnectedness of humanity in facing loss, creating a sense of belonging that can soothe the grieving heart.

Finally, philosophical reflections on life after death invite us to consider the deeper meanings of existence and the nature of our connections. Engaging with these thoughts can help transform grief into a quest for understanding and meaning. By contemplating the legacies of our loved ones and the impact they had on our lives, we can begin to integrate their memories into our ongoing journey. This process allows for growth and healing, encouraging us to honour the past while embracing the present and future. Ultimately, healing practices for the grieving soul are not just about moving on; they are about finding a way to carry our loved ones with us, ensuring that their essence continues to illuminate our paths.

Finding Strength in Faith and Belief

Finding strength in faith and belief can be a transformative journey for those grappling with loss and mourning. When faced with the overwhelming emotions that accompany the departure of a loved one, faith can serve as a guiding light, illuminating a path through the darkness. Belief systems, whether rooted in spiritual traditions, personal philosophies, or cultural practices, can provide a framework for understanding the unexplainable and finding solace in the face of grief. Engaging with these beliefs can empower individuals to navigate their emotional landscapes, drawing on the strength that comes from a deeper connection to something greater than themselves.

Many individuals find comfort in the idea that their loved ones continue to exist in another form, transcending the physical limitations of this world. This belief can foster a sense of ongoing connection, allowing mourners to feel that their relationships are not severed but transformed. Mediumship and spirit communication offer avenues through which individuals can seek messages or signs from those who have passed, reinforcing the belief that love persists beyond death. Such practices can serve as a balm for the heart, helping to bridge the gap between the living and the departed, and providing reassurance that their loved ones are at peace.

Cultural perspectives on the afterlife also play a significant role in shaping how individuals approach grief. Many cultures have rich traditions and rituals that honour the dead, creating spaces for remembrance and celebration. These customs not only validate the experiences of loss but also remind individuals that they are not alone in their sorrow. Participating in these ceremonies can foster a sense of community and shared understanding, allowing mourners to draw strength from collective beliefs and practices that celebrate life, death, and the continuity of the spirit.

Rituals and ceremonies for honouring the departed can provide structure and meaning in the wake of loss. These acts of remembrance serve as tangible expressions of love and respect, allowing individuals to externalize their grief in a way that feels constructive. Whether lighting a candle, creating an altar, or engaging in storytelling, these rituals can become sacred spaces for reflection and connection. They enable mourners to acknowledge their pain while also celebrating the legacy of their loved ones, reinforcing the notion that life continues in new and meaningful ways.

Ultimately, the journey through grief is deeply personal, and the strength found in faith and belief can vary widely from person to person. Embracing this diversity allows for a richer understanding of what it means to mourn and heal. By exploring philosophical reflections on life after death, individuals can cultivate a broader perspective that honours their experiences while opening themselves to the possibility of renewal. In this way, faith and belief become not just sources of comfort, but powerful tools for navigating the complexities of loss, guiding us toward hope, healing, and a deeper appreciation of the bonds that endure beyond the physical realm.

Chapter 3: Mediumship and Spirit Communication

Exploring Mediumship: Connecting with the Beyond

Exploring the realm of mediumship offers a profound avenue for connecting with those we have lost, serving as a bridge between our world and the beyond. For many, the experience of grief can be overwhelming, leading us to seek solace and understanding in various ways. Mediumship, which involves communicating with spirits, can provide comfort and closure, allowing us to feel the presence of our departed loved ones once again. This connection can foster healing and help us navigate the complexities of mourning, reminding us that love transcends even the boundaries of life and death.

As we delve into the intricacies of mediumship, it's essential to recognize that this practice exists within a rich tapestry of cultural beliefs and spiritual traditions. Across the globe, different cultures have their unique perspectives on the afterlife and the means of connecting with spirits. From the ancient rituals of indigenous peoples to contemporary spiritual practices, these traditions highlight a universal human desire to maintain a relationship with those who have passed. Understanding these cultural contexts can deepen our appreciation for the diversity of mediums and their methods, enriching our own experiences as we seek to connect with our loved ones.

Rituals and ceremonies often accompany mediumship, enhancing the experience and providing a structured way to honour the departed. These practices can vary widely, from lighting candles and creating altars to participating in group meditations or ceremonies that celebrate the lives of those we've lost. Such rituals can serve as a powerful reminder that while our loved ones may no longer be physically present, their essence continues to exist in a different realm. Engaging in these meaningful acts can help facilitate a sense of closure and peace, allowing us to feel connected to our loved ones as we navigate our grief.

The psychological effects of loss and mourning can be profound, often leading individuals to seek out various means of healing. Mediumship can play an important role in this process, offering not only messages from the departed but also insights into our own healing journeys. Many individuals report feeling a sense of relief and validation after a mediumship session, as messages from the beyond can provide clarity and understanding about unresolved issues. This connection can also encourage us to embrace our feelings of grief, transforming them into a source of strength and resilience as we honour our loved ones' memories.

Finally, the role of dreams in connecting with the departed cannot be understated. Many people experience vivid dreams featuring their loved ones, often interpreting these encounters as messages or visits from the other side. These dream experiences can be both comforting and enlightening, offering a unique perspective on the nature of life after death. By mirroring on these dreams and their significance, we can further explore our connections to those we have lost, fostering a sense of continuity in our relationships. Ultimately, exploring mediumship and the various ways it manifests in our lives can empower us on our healing paths, encouraging us to embrace the love that continues to surround us, even in the face of loss.

Signs from Loved Ones: Recognising Messages

In the journey of healing from loss, many individuals notice subtle signs that suggest their loved ones are still present in some way. These signs can manifest in various forms—be it a meeting scent, a song that resonates deeply, or an inexplicable feeling of warmth and comfort. Recognizing these messages is not just a comforting notion; it can be a profound aspect of the mourning process. By paying attention to these signs, individuals can create a meaningful connection that transcends the physical absence of their loved ones, fostering a sense of continued relationship and support.

One of the most common ways that loved ones communicate from the beyond is through sensory experiences. The smell of a cherished perfume or cologne, the sudden appearance of a favourite song on the radio, or even the feeling of a gentle breeze can all serve as reminders that our departed are nearby. These experiences often evoke memories, triggering emotions that can be both healing and cathartic. Embracing these occurrences as signs of love can help individuals feel less isolated in their grief and more connected to a larger tapestry of existence that includes both the living and the departed.

In various cultures, the belief in signs from the deceased is woven into the fabric of spiritual practices and rituals. Many traditions encourage individuals to honour their loved ones through ceremonies that invite their presence. This can include lighting candles, creating altars, or participating in specific rites that acknowledge the ongoing bond between the living and the deceased. Such practices not only provide solace but also serve as a reminder that death is not an end, but a transition that allows for continued connection and communication.

Dreams often serve as a powerful conduit for messages from loved ones. Many people report vivid dreams in which they interact with those who have passed, experiencing a sense of peace and closure that may elude them during waking hours. These dreams can be rich in symbolism and emotion, offering insights that help individuals navigate their grief. Keeping a dream journal can be a beneficial practice, allowing individuals to capture the nuances of these experiences and thinking on their meanings over time. This act of remembrance can deepen the understanding of the relationship shared with the departed, reinforcing the notion that love endures beyond death.

Ultimately, recognizing and embracing signs from loved ones is a personal and transformative experience. It encourages individuals to cultivate a mindset of openness and receptivity, allowing them to interpret these messages in ways that resonate with their beliefs and experiences. Whether through spiritual, psychological, or cultural lenses, the act of acknowledging these signs fosters a healing environment where grief can be expressed, understood, and eventually integrated into the journey of life. By honouring the connections that transcend physical existence, individuals can find comfort and hope, paving the way for healing and renewal in the wake of loss.

The Therapeutic Benefits of Spirit Communication

The therapeutic benefits of spirit communication can offer profound solace and healing to those navigating the turbulent waters of grief. For many, the loss of a loved one can feel insurmountable, leading to feelings of isolation and despair. However, engaging in spirit communication—whether through mediumship, dreams, or personal rituals—can provide a sense of connection, understanding, and comfort that transcends physical separation. This connection often reminds individuals that love endures beyond death, fostering a healing environment where emotional wounds can begin to mend.

Spirit communication serves as a bridge between the living and the departed, allowing individuals to express their feelings and unresolved issues. Many people find that speaking to their loved ones, whether through a medium or in quiet reflection, helps them articulate emotions that may have otherwise remained unspoken. This dialogue often opens pathways to forgiveness, closure, and healing, transforming grief into a more manageable experience. The act of reaching out can validate one's feelings and reinforce the belief that the bond shared with the departed continues, offering comfort during the most challenging moments.

Cultural perspectives on the afterlife often shape how individuals approach spirit communication. In many cultures, honouring the deceased through ritual and ceremony is a revered practice that fosters community support and shared grief. These rituals not only provide a structured way to process loss but also create a space for spirit communication to nourish. By participating in these culturally significant practices, individuals can feel a sense of belonging and connection with others who are experiencing similar challenges. This collective experience can be incredibly therapeutic, reinforcing the understanding that one is not alone in their grief journey.

The role of dreams in connecting with loved ones also deserves special mention. Many people report vivid dreams in which they encounter their deceased loved ones, often feeling a sense of peace or clarity upon waking. These dreams can act as powerful healing tools, providing insights or messages that help individuals process their grief. The subconscious mind, in its quest for understanding and resolution, often facilitates these encounters, allowing individuals to explore their emotions in a safe and comforting environment. By embracing these dream experiences, individuals can find hope and reassurance as they navigate their grief.

Finally, philosophical thought on life after death can empower individuals to reshape their understanding of loss. Engaging with the idea that life continues in some form after physical death can provide immense comfort. It encourages individuals to view their grief not as an end but as part of a larger journey. By exploring these philosophical concepts, one can cultivate a sense of purpose and meaning that transcends the pain of loss. This perspective can foster resilience, helping individuals to honour their loved ones while also embracing the beauty of life and the interconnectedness of all beings. In this way, spirit communication becomes not just a means of connecting with the departed but a profound catalyst for healing and personal growth.

Chapter 4: Cultural Perspectives on the Afterlife

Understanding Diverse Beliefs About Death

Understanding diverse beliefs about death is a crucial step in the healing journey for those grappling with loss. Death, a universal experience, is interpreted through myriad lenses shaped by culture, spirituality, and personal experiences. By exploring these varied perspectives, we can nd comfort and connection in our grief, recognizing that while our paths may differ, the emotions we share are profoundly similar. This chapter aims to illuminate these beliefs, offering insights that can foster understanding, empathy, and healing.

Many cultures have rich traditions surrounding death that inform their beliefs about the afterlife and the journey of the soul. For instance, in some Indigenous cultures, death is viewed not as an end but as a transition to a different state of being. This perspective encourages the living to celebrate the deceased's life while acknowledging their ongoing presence in the spiritual realm. Engaging with such cultural perspectives can offer solace, as they remind us that our loved ones may continue to exist in forms we cannot yet see. By embracing these beliefs, we create a bridge between our world and the world beyond, facilitating a sense of connection that transcends physical loss.

Spiritual healing practices often incorporate these diverse beliefs about death, emphasizing the importance of ritual and ceremony. Rituals, whether they are large communal gatherings or intimate personal ceremonies, serve as powerful tools for honouring those who have passed. They allow us to express our grief, celebrate lives, and acknowledge the impact of loss on our own spiritual journeys. By participating in these rituals, we can observe a sense of closure and healing, recognizing that our loved ones remain part of our lives through memories, stories, and the love they instilled in us.

Mediumship and spirit communication offer another avenue for understanding our relationship with death. Many individuals discover comfort in connecting with a medium, who can facilitate communication with the departed. This process can validate feelings of loss and provide reassurance that our loved ones are still present in some form. Such experiences can also challenge our perceptions of reality, inviting us to think on the nature of existence and our connections to one another. By exploring these interactions, we can cultivate a deeper understanding of our loved ones' journeys beyond the physical realm, which may alleviate some of the pain associated with their absence.

Ultimately, understanding diverse beliefs about death empowers us to navigate our grief with compassion and resilience. As we learn from various cultural and spiritual perspectives, we can foster a more profound appreciation for the complexities of life and death. This journey is not about erasing our pain but rather embracing it as part of the human experience. By recognizing that our feelings are shared across cultures and histories, we can realise strength in community and shared understanding. In this way, our exploration of death and what lies beyond can lead us toward healing, helping us honour the memories of our loved ones while nurturing our own spirits in the process.

How Culture Shapes Our Grieving Process

Grief is a universal experience, yet the ways in which we process this profound emotion are deeply influenced by cultural beliefs and practices. Each culture provides a framework through which individuals interpret loss, shaping not only their feelings but also their rituals and responses. Understanding the cultural variances in grieving can illuminate our own paths through sorrow, helping us to navigate the complex emotional landscape that follows the

The Healing Path: Understanding Psychological Effects of Loss and Mourning

death of a loved one. By exploring these cultural dimensions, we can observe solace in shared practices and beliefs, reminding ourselves that we are not alone in our grief.

Rituals and ceremonies play a critical role in how cultures honour the departed and cope with loss. From elaborate funerals to intimate gatherings, these practices are designed to acknowledge the reality of death while providing a supportive environment for the bereaved. In many cultures, rituals serve as a bridge to the spiritual realm, fostering a sense of connection with those who have passed. These ceremonies often include elements that encourage communal support, allowing individuals to share their experiences and emotions. Engaging in such rituals can offer a sense of closure and a pathway to healing, reminding us that grief is not solely a personal journey but a communal one as well.

Cultural perspectives on the afterlife also shape our grieving processes. Beliefs about what happens after death can influence how individuals cope with loss. For instance, some cultures hold onto the belief in reincarnation, which can provide comfort in the notion that life continues in another form. Others may embrace the idea of a heavenly reunion, fostering hope and encouraging the bereaved to celebrate the life of the deceased rather than solely mourn their absence. By understanding and embracing these cultural beliefs, individuals can find new meaning in their grief, transforming it into a source of strength and resilience.

The psychological effects of loss are universally profound, but culture offers unique coping mechanisms that can aid in the healing process. For instance, in certain cultures, storytelling and sharing memories serve as powerful tools for processing grief, allowing the bereaved to reflect on the life of their loved ones and maintain a connection with them. Engaging in these practices can facilitate emotional expression and foster a sense of continuity, making it easier for individuals to navigate their sorrow. By incorporating cultural elements into our grieving process, we can utilize these tools to foster healing, transforming our pain into a celebration of life and love.

Ultimately, recognizing the role of culture in our grieving process encourages us to embrace a more holistic approach to healing. By honouring diverse perspectives and practices surrounding loss, we can create a rich tapestry of understanding that supports our journeys through grief. Whether through ritual, belief, or shared stories, cultural frameworks offer pathways for connection and healing, reminding us that love transcends even death. As we navigate our own grief, let us draw strength from these cultural insights, allowing them to guide us on our healing path and connect us to the enduring spirit of those we have lost.

Lessons from Global Traditions in Mourning

In exploring the profound impact of loss and mourning, we discover that global traditions offer invaluable lessons that can guide us through our grief. Across cultures, mourning practices encapsulate the universal human experience of loss while also honouring the memory of those who have passed. These rituals, steeped in history and spirituality, provide pathways to healing that resonate deeply in the hearts of the bereaved. By understanding and integrating these varied traditions, we can cultivate a more holistic approach to our own mourning process.

One of the most striking lessons from global mourning traditions is the emphasis on community support. In many cultures, grief is not borne in isolation but shared among family, friends, and the community. This collective mourning allows individuals to feel supported and understood, helping to alleviate the weight of their sorrow. For instance, the practice of sitting shiva in Jewish culture encourages the bereaved to surround themselves with loved ones, fostering an environment where shared sadness transforms into collective healing. Engaging with our communities during times of loss can remind us that we are never truly alone in our grief.

Rituals serve as powerful tools for honouring the departed and facilitating the grieving process. Various cultures employ distinct ceremonies that can range from elaborate funerals to simple, intimate gatherings. These rituals not only pay tribute to the lives of those we've lost but also create a structured environment for expressing emotions. The Day of the Dead in Mexico exempli es this beautifully, as families gather to celebrate and remember their ancestors, blending mourning with joyful remembrance. By incorporating rituals into our own grieving processes, we can create meaningful moments that acknowledge our pain while also celebrating the love that remains.

Another crucial aspect of mourning traditions is the belief in an afterlife or ongoing connection with the deceased. Many cultures hold that death is not an end but rather a transition, allowing the spirit to continue its journey. This perspective can provide solace to those grieving, reinforcing the idea that their loved ones remain a part of their lives in a different form.
Mediumship practices, prevalent in various cultures, allow individuals to seek communication with the departed, fostering a sense of connection that transcends physical loss. Embracing these beliefs can empower us to asset comfort in the idea that our loved ones are still present in some capacity, guiding us through our sorrow.

Ultimately, the lessons from global mourning traditions remind us that grief is a deeply personal yet shared experience. Each culture offers unique insights into the emotional, psychological, and spiritual dimensions of loss. By respecting these diverse practices and philosophies, we can asset a richer understanding of our own paths through mourning. It is a journey that not only honours those we have lost but also allows us to emerge with renewed strength, a deeper appreciation for life, and a connection to the enduring bonds of love that transcend even death.

Chapter 5: Rituals and Ceremonies for Honouring the Departed

The Power of Ritual in Healing

Rituals have long served as a bridge between the living and the departed, offering a structured way to process grief and connect with the spiritual realm. For those navigating the tumultuous waters of loss, engaging in meaningful rituals can foster a sense of belonging and purpose. These practices not only honour the memory of loved ones but also create a space for healing, allowing individuals to express their emotions and mirror on their relationships. By incorporating rituals into the grieving process, we can transform sorrow into a pathway for spiritual growth, encouraging a deeper understanding of both life and death.

From the simple act of lighting a candle in remembrance to elaborate ceremonies that celebrate a loved one's life, rituals provide a tangible way to acknowledge loss. They serve as a reminder that the connection with the departed continues, even after physical separation. In various cultures, rituals are imbued with symbolic meanings, allowing participants to express their grief in ways that resonate with their beliefs and values. This diversity in practices underscores the universal need to honour those who have passed, reinforcing the idea that, while grief is deeply personal, it also connects us to a larger community of shared experiences.

The psychological effects of engaging in ritual practices during mourning can be profound. Rituals create a framework that helps to organize the chaos of emotions, providing a sense of stability and control in a time of upheaval. They invite uncovering and encourage individuals to share their stories, creating an environment where healing can occur. This communal aspect of rituals allows mourners to feel supported and understood, fostering connections with others who have faced similar losses. The act of coming together, whether in a small gathering or a larger community event, can transform isolation into solidarity, enabling individuals to navigate their grief alongside others.

Furthermore, rituals can enhance the process of spirit communication, allowing individuals to feel closer to their departed loved ones. Many perceive comfort in practices that invite messages from the spiritual realm, whether through mediumship, dreams, or personal observation. By intentionally creating space for these connections, individuals can experience moments of solace and reassurance that transcend the physical boundaries of life and death. The belief that our loved ones are still present, in some form, can be incredibly healing, offering hope and a renewed sense of purpose during grief.

Ultimately, the power of ritual lies in its ability to honour the past while nurturing the healing journey toward the future. Each act of remembrance, whether grand or simple, contributes to the ongoing process of reconciliation with loss. By embracing rituals as essential tools for healing, we invite a deeper exploration of our relationships with those we have lost and with ourselves. In doing so, we affirm the enduring bond of love that transcends the veil of death, allowing us to move forward with both grace and strength, cherishing the memories of those who continue to walk alongside us in spirit.

Creating Personal Ceremonies of Remembrance

Creating personal ceremonies of remembrance can be a deeply transformative way to honour the memory of a loved one while facilitating your own healing journey. These ceremonies serve as a bridge between the physical world and the spiritual realm, providing a sacred space where you can express your grief, celebrate your loved one's life, and connect with the essence of their spirit. By infusing personal touches into the ceremony, you can create a unique experience that resonates with your heart and fosters a sense of connection that transcends loss.

Begin by reflecting on what made your loved one unique. Consider their favourite places, hobbies, or cherished memories. These elements can be woven into the fabric of your ceremony, allowing you to create a meaningful tribute that is deeply personal. Perhaps you might choose to hold the ceremony in a location that was significant to them, or incorporate their favourite music, poetry, or photographs. Each detail contributes to a rich tapestry of remembrance, helping you to not only honour their life but also to express your emotions in a safe and supportive environment.

In addition to personal elements, consider incorporating spiritual practices that resonate with you. Many cultures around the world have rituals designed to honour the deceased and facilitate communication with the spirit realm. Lighting candles, creating an altar, or engaging in meditation can serve as powerful tools in your ceremony. These practices not only invite a sense of peace but also create a channel for you to connect with the spiritual essence of your loved one, offering comfort and clarity in your grieving process.

As you design your personal ceremony, invite others who share in your grief to participate. This communal aspect can be healing, as it allows for the sharing of stories and memories, fostering a sense of togetherness in the face of loss. Engaging in group activities, such as sharing a meal, planting a tree, or participating in a group meditation, can further strengthen those bonds of love and remembrance. Together, you create a supportive space where everyone feels validated in their emotions, reinforcing the idea that grief is not a solitary journey but a shared experience.

Finally, embrace the flexibility of your ceremony. There is no right or wrong way to honour your loved one; what matters most is that it resonates with your heart and speaks to your unique relationship. Allow the ceremony to evolve organically, adapting to your feelings and insights as they arise. This dynamic approach not only honours the memory of your loved one but also acknowledges your own journey of healing. By creating a personal ceremony of remembrance, you take a important step towards understanding the psychological effects of loss, embracing the complexity of mourning, and fostering a deeper connection with both the past and the spiritual realm.

Community Practices and Their Impact

Community practices play a crucial role in the healing journey following loss and mourning. When loved ones come together to share their grief, they not only foster a sense of belonging but also create a collective space for healing. These gatherings can take on various forms, from informal meetings with friends to structured support groups led by grief counsellors. In this context, shared experiences become a powerful tool for understanding and processing the emotional turmoil that follows the death of a loved one. The act of coming together allows individuals to articulate their feelings, validate each other's experiences, and begin to rebuild their lives in the presence of compassionate witnesses.

Spiritual healing often finds its roots in community practices that honour the departed while offering support to those left behind. Rituals and ceremonies, whether traditional or uniquely tailored to the individuals involved, serve as vital expressions of love and remembrance. These practices can provide a framework for participants to express their grief, celebrate the lives of those who have passed, and foster a connection that transcends physical absence. Whether through candlelight vigils, memorial services, or cultural rites, these communal activities create a sacred space where the living can engage with their memories and emotions, thus facilitating a deeper understanding of their loss.

In many cultures, the afterlife is viewed through a lens that emphasizes ongoing relationships between the living and the deceased. Community practices often incorporate spiritual beliefs about the afterlife, which can offer comfort and a sense of continuity. For instance, mediumship and spirit communication can be integral to community gatherings, allowing individuals to seek solace through messages or signs from their loved ones. These practices can alleviate feelings of isolation by affirming the belief that connections remain intact despite physical separation. Such perspectives encourage individuals to explore their own beliefs about life after death, enriching their personal healing journeys.

The psychological effects of loss can be overwhelming, but community practices provide a supportive environment for individuals to navigate their grief. Engaging with others who share similar experiences fosters empathy and understanding, which can be transformative. Additionally, these gatherings often encourage storytelling, allowing individuals to reflect on their loved ones' lives and the impact they had. Such reflections can shift focus away from the pain of absence toward a celebration of legacy, helping individuals seek meaning in their grief. This sense of purpose can be instrumental in healing, as it helps individuals integrate their loss into the larger tapestry of their lives.

Finally, the role of dreams in connecting with loved ones is another fascinating aspect of community practices. Many cultures embrace the idea that dreams can serve as a bridge to the other side, offering comfort and messages from those who have passed. Sharing these dream experiences within a community can validate feelings and provide insights into the grieving process. By discussing dreams and honouring the messages received, individuals can find reassurance and a renewed sense of hope. Ultimately, the collective practices of mourning serve not only to honour those we have lost but also to reinforce the bonds of community, love, and healing that endure beyond loss.

Chapter 6: Psychological Effects of Loss and Mourning

The Emotional Toll of Grief

The journey through grief is deeply personal, often marked by a spectrum of emotions that can feel overwhelming. For many, the emotional toll of grief manifests not only in sadness but also in anger, guilt, confusion, and even moments of joy as memories resurface. Understanding these emotions is crucial for anyone navigating the tumultuous waters of loss. Recognizing that grief is not a linear process, but rather a series of waves that ebb and ow, can offer solace. Embracing the complexity of these feelings allows us to honour our loved ones while also caring for ourselves during sorrow.

In the realm of spiritual healing and grief counselling, acknowledging the emotional toll is the first step towards healing. Professional counsellors often emphasize the importance of expressing feelings rather than suppressing them. This expression can take many forms, from talking to a trusted friend to engaging in creative outlets like art or writing. By giving voice to our grief, we can begin to process our emotions, creating a space where healing can take root. Encouragement from those who have walked similar paths can remind us that we are not alone in our struggles, and that it's perfectly acceptable to feel a wide range of emotions during this time.

Mediumship and spirit communication offer an additional layer of understanding to the emotional experiences tied to grief. Many individuals find comfort in the belief that their loved ones remain present in spirit, providing reassurance and support from beyond this world. Engaging with a medium or participating in spirit communication practices can facilitate connections that help soothe the emotional burden of loss. These experiences can be profoundly validating, allowing individuals to feel a sense of peace and closure, while also affirming the love that transcends physical absence.

Cultural perspectives on the afterlife contribute significantly to how grief is experienced and expressed. Different cultures have their own rituals and ceremonies for honouring the departed, which can provide a framework for individuals to navigate their grief. Engaging in these time-honoured practices not only serves to honour those who have passed but also fosters communal support and understanding. Such rituals can transform the emotional toll of grief into a shared experience, reminding us that while loss is deeply personal, it is also a universal aspect of the human condition that connects us all.

Lastly, exploring the psychological effects of loss and mourning reveals that grief can also lead to profound personal growth. Although the emotional toll can feel heavy, it often paves the way for a deeper understanding of life, love, and purpose. As we grapple with the questions surrounding life after death and the importance of our connections, we may find new insights and perspectives that enrich our lives. In this light, grief can be seen not only as a painful journey but also as an opportunity for transformation, inviting us to honour our loved ones while embracing the potential for healing and renewal in our own lives.

Coping Mechanisms: Healthy vs. Unhealthy

Coping mechanisms are essential tools in navigating the tumultuous waters of grief and loss. When faced with the profound emotional upheaval that accompanies the death of a loved one, individuals often seek ways to manage their feelings and find solace. Understanding the distinction between healthy and unhealthy coping mechanisms can significantly impact the healing journey. Healthy coping strategies allow individuals to process their emotions in constructive ways, fostering resilience and growth. In contrast, unhealthy coping mechanisms can lead to further emotional distress and hinder the path toward acceptance and healing.

The Healing Path: Understanding Psychological Effects of Loss and Mourning

Healthy coping mechanisms often involve embracing one's feelings and allowing space for grief. This may include engaging in spiritual practices such as meditation, prayer, or participating in rituals that honour the departed. These activities not only provide comfort but also create a sense of connection with the spiritual realm, where loved ones may still reside. Engaging in supportive conversations with friends, family, or professional grief counsellors can also be a powerful means of processing emotions. Such interactions validate feelings and foster a sense of community, reminding individuals they are not alone in their grief.

On the other hand, unhealthy coping strategies often manifest as avoidance, denial, or self-destructive behaviors. Some individuals might resort to substance abuse, isolating themselves from others, or suppressing their emotions in an attempt to alleviate their pain. While these behaviors may provide temporary relief, they ultimately prolong the grieving process and can lead to deeper psychological issues. It is crucial to recognize these patterns and seek healthier alternatives that promote healing rather than hinder it. Understanding that grief is a natural response to loss can empower individuals to embrace their emotions rather than shy away from them.

Cultural perspectives on mourning and the afterlife can also play a signi cant role in shaping coping mechanisms. Different cultures have unique rituals and ceremonies designed to honor the departed, which can be invaluable in the grieving process. Participating in these traditions not only offers a structured way to express grief but also connects individuals to their heritage and spiritual beliefs. By incorporating these cultural practices into their coping strategies, individuals can nd comfort and meaning in their loss, reinforcing the idea that love transcends physical existence.

Ultimately, the journey through grief is deeply personal, and the coping mechanisms that work for one person may not resonate with another. Encouraging individuals to explore various approaches—whether through spiritual connection, community support, or self-re ection—can help them discover what feels most healing. Finding a balance between acknowledging pain and seeking joy in memories can be a powerful act of love for those who have passed. By fostering healthy coping mechanisms, individuals can navigate their grief with grace, ultimately transforming their loss into a profound journey of healing and understanding.

Seeking Professional Support

Seeking professional support during the journey of grief can be a profound step toward healing and understanding the complex emotions that arise after a loss. For many, the pain of losing a loved one can feel isolating and overwhelming. However, engaging with professionals who specialize in grief counselling or spiritual healing can provide not only comfort but also valuable tools for navigating this challenging terrain. These experts offer insights that can help

The Healing Path: Understanding Psychological Effects of Loss and Mourning

individuals process their grief in a way that honours both the departed and their own emotional needs.

Grief counsellors are trained to understand the psychological effects of loss and mourning. They can help individuals explore their feelings in a safe, supportive environment. This professional guidance can be particularly beneficial for those who feel lost in their grief or struggle to articulate their emotions. Counsellors can introduce practices such as journaling or mindfulness, which encourage individuals to mirror on their experiences and connect with their inner selves. These methods can foster a sense of agency and clarity, empowering the grieving person to confront their feelings rather than shy away from them.

For those inclined towards spiritual healing, engaging with mediums or practitioners of spirit communication can also be a profound source of comfort. These professionals offer a unique perspective on the afterlife and can facilitate connections with departed loved ones, providing reassurance that the bond remains intact. Many find solace in knowing that their loved ones continue to exist in some form, and these experiences can bring closure and peace. The process of connecting with a medium can also serve as a ritual, a meaningful act that honours the departed and reinforces the belief in a continuing relationship beyond physical existence.

Cultural perspectives on the afterlife can vary widely, and exploring these views can enrich one's understanding of grief. Different cultures have unique rituals and ceremonies for honouring the departed, which can serve as powerful tools for healing. Engaging with these practices can help individuals feel a sense of belonging and community, reinforcing the idea that grief is a shared human experience. By seeking professional support in this area, individuals can learn to incorporate these cultural rituals into their own grieving process, creating a personalized path that resonates with their beliefs and values.

Ultimately, the journey through grief is highly personal and often requires a multifaceted approach. Embracing professional support—whether through counselling, spiritual practices, or community rituals—can provide invaluable assistance along this healing path. Each step taken toward understanding and processing the loss is a step toward honouring the memory of the loved one while also nurturing one's own emotional well-being. In seeking this support, individuals can seek not only solace but also a renewed sense of hope as they navigate the complexities of mourning.

Chapter 7: Historical Accounts of Spirit Encounters

Stories of Connection: The Living and the Departed

In the journey of healing from loss, stories of connection between the living and the departed serve as powerful reminders of the enduring bonds we share with those who have passed. These narratives often illuminate the profound ways in which love transcends the boundaries of physical existence. For many, the experience of feeling a loved one's presence or receiving a sign from them can be both comforting and transformative. Such connections can manifest in various forms, from subtle synchronicities to vivid dreams, fostering a sense of continued companionship that aids in the grieving process.

Mediumship and spirit communication have long been avenues through which individuals seek to reconnect with those they have lost. Many discover solace in the insights offered by mediums, who act as conduits between the living and the departed. These encounters often provide not only closure but also reassurance that our loved ones are at peace and still part of our lives in some way. The stories shared by those who have experienced such connections highlight the universal desire to maintain relationships beyond the physical realm. These experiences remind us that love is not con ned to the limits of life and death; rather, it evolves and adapts, creating new pathways for communication.

Cultural perspectives on the afterlife further enrich our understanding of these connections. Different traditions offer unique insights into how we can honour our departed loved ones and maintain connections with them. Rituals and ceremonies, whether intimate or communal, serve as powerful expressions of love and remembrance. They provide a structured way to acknowledge grief while simultaneously celebrating the lives of those who have passed. For many cultures, these practices are not just about mourning but also about affirming the belief that our loved ones continue to exist in a different form, encouraging us to engage with them through memory and tradition.

The role of dreams in connecting with loved ones is particularly fascinating, as many individuals report vivid experiences where the boundaries between the living and the departed blur. In these dreams, the departed often convey messages of love, guidance, or even humour, offering comfort to those who are grieving. Such experiences can be deeply healing, allowing individuals to process their feelings of loss while fostering a continued relationship with the loved one. These dream encounters validate the idea that our loved ones are still present in our lives, urging us to embrace the memories and lessons they imparted.

Philosophical show itself on life after death encourage us to ponder the nature of existence and the legacies we leave behind. As we grapple with the psychological effects of loss and mourning, these reflections can inspire a sense of purpose in our grief. By sharing stories of connection, we honour the lives of our departed loved ones and reaffirm that their impact on our lives endures. In the tapestry of life, connections woven through love, memory, and spirit remind us that while we may experience physical separation, the essence of those we cherish remains intertwined with our journey, guiding us toward healing and acceptance.

The Influence of Historical Context on Beliefs

The influence of historical context on beliefs surrounding loss and mourning is profound and multifaceted. Throughout history, societies have developed unique frameworks for understanding death and the afterlife, shaped by cultural, religious, and philosophical inpact. These frameworks often dictate how individuals experience grief and engage in healing practices. For loved ones navigating their own grief, recognizing the historical context of their beliefs can be a powerful way to foster understanding and acceptance, allowing them to honour their feelings while also exploring the broader narratives that have shaped their perspectives on loss.

In various cultures, historical events have shaped communal and individual beliefs about death. For instance, periods of war, plague, or social upheaval often led to shifts in how people perceive the afterlife and the rituals associated with mourning. During the Black Death, for example, many European communities turned to religious explanations for death, emphasizing the need for penance and the hope of eternal life. By understanding this historical ascendancy, individuals can gain insight into their own grief responses and the rituals they may choose to engage in. This understanding can pave the way for healing, integrating personal pain with the collective experiences of humanity.

Moreover, the evolution of spiritual beliefs over time contributes to how individuals process loss. As societies have transitioned from pagan beliefs to organized religions and, more recently, to secular perspectives, the ways in which people connect with the departed have also changed. Mediumship and spirit communication, once widely accepted practices, have actuated in popularity, reflecting the cultural zeitgeist. Loved ones exploring these elements may find comfort in recognizing that their desire for connection with the deceased is part of a long-standing human tradition, one that transcends time and space. This realization can provide solace, reinforcing the notion that seeking connection and understanding in loss is a deeply rooted human instinct.

Rituals and ceremonies, too, play a crucial role in how grief is experienced and expressed. Historical contexts dictate which rituals are honoured in different cultures, from elaborate funeral rites to simple moments of remembrance. These practices not only serve to honour the departed but also to guide the bereaved through their mourning process. Acknowledging the historical significance of these rituals can empower individuals to create their own personalized ceremonies, drawing from both tradition and their unique experiences. By blending past practices with personal meaning, loved ones can cultivate a healing environment that respects both their grief and the cultural narratives that shape their beliefs.

Ultimately, understanding the historical context of beliefs surrounding loss can lead to a greater appreciation for the diversity of grief experiences. It encourages an open dialogue about death, mourning, and the afterlife, allowing loved ones to explore various perspectives without judgment. This exploration can foster a sense of community among those who share similar experiences and beliefs, offering a supportive network for healing. In navigating the complexities of grief, individuals can draw strength from the rich tapestry of historical impact, finding hope and healing in the shared human experience of loss.

Learning from the Past: Insights into Mourning

Mourning is a universal experience, one that transcends cultures, beliefs, and time. Throughout history, people have navigated the complex waters of grief, often discovering profound insights that can guide us in our own journeys. By understanding how different communities have historically approached mourning, we can glean valuable lessons that resonate with our current experiences. Embracing these insights allows us to honour our loved ones while also recognizing the shared humanity in our collective grief.

Many cultures have created rich rituals and ceremonies to commemorate the deceased, reflecting their beliefs about the afterlife and the continued presence of the loved ones in spirit. These practices serve not only as a means of honouring those who have passed but also as a way for the living to express their sorrow and seek solace. Engaging in rituals—whether lighting a candle, creating a memory altar, or participating in community gatherings— can provide a tangible connection to those we have lost. Such acts remind us that mourning is not a solitary journey; it is a communal experience that fosters connection and healing.

Historical accounts of spirit encounters reveal a fascinating dimension to the mourning process. Many individuals have reported experiences that suggest a continued relationship with their loved ones after death. These encounters can manifest in various ways, from dreams that carry messages to moments of synchronicity that evoke a sense of presence. By exploring these narratives, we can shift our perspective on grief, recognizing that while loss is deeply painful, it can coexist with the belief in an enduring connection that transcends physical existence. This understanding can bring comfort and hope, encouraging us to remain open to the signs and messages from the other side.

The psychological effects of loss can be overwhelming, yet they can also lead to profound personal growth and transformation. Mourning is not merely a state of sorrow; it is an opportunity for reflection and introspection. As we process our grief, we often confront our beliefs about life, death, and what lies beyond. This exploration can lead to philosophical thinking that deepen our understanding of existence and our place within it. Embracing the lessons of mourning can empower us to see meaning in our loss, allowing us to honour our loved ones by living fully and authentically in their memory.

In conclusion, the past offers a wealth of insights into the mourning process, guiding us through our grief with wisdom and compassion. By learning from the rituals, experiences, and thinking of those who have come before us, we can cultivate a deeper understanding of our own feelings of loss. Mourning is not just an end but a beginning—a chance to foster resilience, connect with our loved ones in new ways, and ultimately heal. As we walk this path, let us remember that we are not alone; we carry the love and lessons of those who have touched our lives, guiding us toward a brighter, more compassionate future.

Chapter 8: The Role of Dreams in Connecting with Loved Ones

Understanding Dream Symbolism in Grief

Dreams can serve as profound vessels for our emotions, especially during periods of grief. When we lose someone dear to us, the subconscious mind often processes complex feelings through dreams, transforming raw anguish into symbolic narratives. These dreams can illuminate our inner world, revealing not only our sorrow but also our hopes, fears, and unresolved matters concerning our loved ones. By understanding the symbolism within these dreams, we can navigate the tumultuous waters of grief with greater clarity and compassion, ultimately fostering healing and connection.

In many cultures, dreams are perceived as bridges to the spiritual realm. They provide a unique opportunity for communication with those who have passed. Symbols such as light, water, or specific objects may emerge in our dreams, each carrying distinct meanings that reflect our relationship with the departed. For instance, dreaming of water often signifies emotional release or transformation, while the presence of light can represent guidance or reassurance from a loved one. By exploring these symbols, we gain insights into our emotional state and the messages our subconscious is attempting to convey, nurturing a sense of peace and understanding.

Grief dreams can also serve as a space for dialogue with those we have lost. Many individuals report experiencing vivid encounters with their loved ones during sleep, where conversations or shared moments unfold. These dreams can be comforting, offering closure or clarity on unresolved issues. Embracing these experiences as meaningful encounters because the imagination allows us to honour the connection we still share with our loved ones. This perspective encourages us to hold space for both our pain and the enduring bonds of love, reminding us that grief is not a linear process, but a complex journey led with opportunities for healing.

The interpretation of dream symbolism is often influenced by cultural beliefs and personal experiences. Different cultures have rich traditions surrounding dreams, viewing them as sacred messages or omens. By examining these cultural perspectives, we can deepen our understanding of our own dreams in the context of grief. Integrating rituals or practices from various traditions —such as journaling about our dreams or seeking guidance from a spiritual counsellor—can enhance our connection to the dream world. This cultural lens not only validates our experiences but also enriches our healing process, allowing us to draw strength from the collective wisdom of those who have traversed similar paths.

Ultimately, understanding dream symbolism in grief opens a pathway to healing that transcends traditional mourning practices. It invites us to engage with our emotions in a holistic manner, recognizing that dreams can be both a reflection of our psychological state and a means of connecting with the spiritual dimensions of our loss. By embracing our dreams as powerful tools for understanding and healing, we can navigate the complex landscape of grief with newfound insight and resilience. In doing so, we honour not only our loved ones but also the profound journey of life and death that binds us all together.

Lucid Dreams and Messages from Beyond

Lucid dreams, where the dreamer is aware of their dreaming state and can often control the dream narrative, have long been regarded as a profound bridge between the conscious and unconscious mind. For many, these dreams can become a powerful tool for connection with loved ones who have passed away. In the context of grief, experiencing lucid dreams may provide solace, offering unique messages or insights from those we miss dearly. This phenomenon holds particular significance in spiritual healing, as it often fosters a deeper understanding of loss and enables individuals to feel a sense of closeness to their departed loved ones.

Many cultures around the world have revered dreams as a medium of communication with the spiritual realm. Historical accounts highlight how indigenous tribes and various spiritual traditions have regarded dreams as sacred, often interpreting them as messages from ancestors or spirits. These cultural perspectives underscore the belief that the boundaries between life and death are not as rigid as they may appear. Engaging with lucid dreams can thus serve as a healing ritual, allowing individuals to honour their loved ones while exploring the depths of their own emotional experiences surrounding grief.

Moreover, the psychological effects of loss can often manifest in dreams, becoming a canvas for unresolved feelings and unexpressed words. Lucid dreaming offers a unique opportunity to confront these emotions directly. By inviting the departed into the dream space, individuals can seek closure or understanding, asking questions that may linger in their waking lives. This interactive dialogue can be a source of comfort, transforming grief into a more manageable experience and allowing the dreamer to cultivate a sense of peace and acceptance.

The role of dreams in connecting with loved ones extends beyond mere personal experience; it resonates with a broader philosophical inquiry into life after death. Many find that these interactions within the dream state challenge conventional notions of mortality, suggesting that love and connection transcend the physical realm. This insight can inspire a profound shift in perspective, encouraging individuals to embrace the idea that their loved ones continue to exist in a different form, guiding and supporting them even after physical separation.

Incorporating rituals and ceremonies that honour these dream connections can further deepen the healing process. Whether through journaling about the lucid experiences, sharing them with a grief counsellor, or participating in community gatherings that celebrate the departed, these practices can solidify the bonds formed in the dream world. Ultimately, lucid dreams can serve as both a comforting embrace and a pathway to healing, reminding us that love does not end with death and that the connections we cherish can evolve into new forms of understanding and acceptance.

Techniques for Enhancing Dream Connections

In the journey of healing from loss, dreams often serve as a profound bridge connecting us with our departed loved ones. The realm of dreams offers a unique opportunity for spiritual connection and understanding, fostering a

sense of ongoing relationship with those who have passed. By intentionally enhancing our dream connections, we can open our hearts and minds to deeper messages, comfort, and guidance that may come through in the dream state. This subchapter explores several techniques designed to strengthen these connections, inviting you to embrace the spiritual and emotional richness that lies within your dreams.

The Healing Path: Understanding Psychological Effects of Loss and Mourning

One effective technique for enhancing dream connections is the practice of setting intentions before sleep. As you prepare for rest, take a moment to quiet your mind and focus on the loved one you wish to connect with. You might choose to speak your intention aloud or write it down in a journal, clearly expressing your desire to receive guidance or messages in your dreams. This act of intention-setting serves as a powerful signal to your subconscious, encouraging it to be receptive to the presence of your loved one during your dream state. With time and practice, you may find that your dreams become more vivid, meaningful, and directly related to your emotional needs.

Another powerful method involves creating a sacred space for your dreams. This can be as simple as arranging your bedroom to be more inviting and calming or incorporating elements that remind you of your loved one—such as photographs, heirlooms, or items infused with their essence. Consider lighting a candle or burning incense before sleep to create an atmosphere conducive to spiritual communication. By surrounding yourself with these meaningful items, you cultivate an environment that honours the memory of your loved one and invites their presence into your dreams, making it easier for you to connect with them on a deeper level.

In addition to these practices, keeping a dream journal can be an invaluable tool for enhancing dream connections. Upon waking, take a few moments to jot down any dreams you recall, no matter how fragmented or obscure. Over time, patterns may emerge that offer insights into your emotional state and your relationship with your departed loved one. Not only does this practice help you remember your dreams more vividly, but it also encourages reflection and interpretation, allowing you to discern the messages and themes that arise. This ongoing dialogue with your dreams enriches the grieving process, transforming your memories into a source of comfort and understanding.

Lastly, consider integrating rituals and ceremonies into your routine that honour your loved one's memory. These practices can provide a focal point for your intentions and desires to connect with them during your dreams. Whether it's lighting a candle, creating a memory altar, or participating in community rituals, these acts of remembrance can enhance your spiritual connection. By establishing a meaningful context for your dreaming experience, you invite your loved one to visit you more readily, nurturing the bond that transcends physical existence. Embrace these techniques with an open heart and allow the healing power of your dreams to guide you through the landscape of grief toward a renewed sense of peace and connection.

Chapter 9: Philosophical Reflections on Life After Death

Contemplating Existence Beyond This Life

Contemplating existence beyond this life invites us to explore the profound questions that arise when we face the loss of a loved one. This journey often leads us to see not only on our personal beliefs but also on the collective understanding of what lies beyond. Engaging with these questions can be a source of comfort and healing, allowing us to connect with our loved ones in ways that transcend the physical world. As we navigate the complexities of grief, we may seek that contemplating the afterlife becomes a crucial aspect of our healing process, offering us hope and a deeper understanding of our experiences.

Spiritual healing plays a significant role in how we cope with loss. Many individuals turn to practices such as mediumship and spirit communication to bridge the gap between the living and the departed. These interactions can provide reassurance that our loved ones continue to exist in some form, fostering a sense of connection that transcends time and space. Engaging with mediums or practicing personal forms of communication can help alleviate feelings of isolation and despair, reminding us that love does not end with physical separation. This belief in ongoing existence can be a powerful tool for healing, allowing us to honour our loved ones while also nurturing our own spirits.

Cultural perspectives on the afterlife further enrich our understanding of existence beyond this life. Various traditions offer unique insights into what happens after death, from reincarnation in Eastern philosophies to the concept of heaven in Western religions. Exploring these diverse beliefs can provide comfort and inspire us to reflect on our own views. Rituals and ceremonies rooted in cultural practices often serve as vital expressions of love, helping us to honour and celebrate the lives of those we have lost. By incorporating these rituals into our mourning process, we not only pay tribute to our loved ones but also embrace a sense of community and shared understanding, which can be deeply healing.

The psychological effects of loss and mourning can sometimes lead us to question our beliefs about existence beyond this life. We may grapple with fear, uncertainty, and doubt as we confront the nullity of death. However, embracing philosophical reflections on life after death can offer clarity and solace. Engaging with existential questions encourages us to consider the legacy our loved ones leave behind and how they're influence continues to shape our lives. This contemplation can shift our focus from the pain of loss to the profound impact of love, inspiring us to carry forward the values and lessons imparted by those who have departed.

Lastly, the role of dreams in connecting with our loved ones cannot be overlooked. Many people report experiencing vivid dreams of those they have lost, often feeling a sense of presence and communication that brings comfort. These dreams can serve as a reminder that our connections are not severed by death; rather, they evolve into new forms. By remaining open to these experiences, we can gain insights into our grief and find peace in the notion that love endures. Ultimately, contemplating existence beyond this life encourages us to embrace a holistic view of love, loss, and connection, paving the way for healing and a deeper appreciation of the journeys we all share.

The Meaning of Loss in the Cycle of Life

The experience of loss is an intrinsic part of the human journey, woven deeply into the fabric of life itself. In "The Healing Path: Understanding Psychological Effects of Loss and Mourning," we explore how the meaning of loss transcends mere absence, inviting us to re ect on the profound connections we share with those who have departed. This chapter delves into the spiritual and psychological dimensions of loss, illuminating how it can serve as a catalyst for growth, understanding, and healing. Each sorrow can lead us to a deeper appreciation of life, encouraging us to embrace our emotions and find solace in the memories of our loved ones.

Loss often prompts us to confront our beliefs about existence, mortality, and the afterlife. Different cultures offer varied perspectives on this transition, enriching our understanding of what it means to lose someone dear. From the rituals of honouring the departed to the comforting practices of spirit communication, these customs serve not only as tools for mourning but also as pathways to spiritual healing. They remind us that death is not an end but a transformation, encouraging us to celebrate the essence of those we have lost rather than solely grieving their absence.

Psychologically, the effects of loss can be profound yet transformative. Mourning is a natural process, one that allows us to navigate the complexities of our emotions and rediscover our sense of self. The journey through grief may be fraught with pain, but within that pain lies the potential for renewal. Many believe that engaging in rituals or ceremonies becomes a vital part of their healing, creating a sacred space to honour their loved ones. These acts can facilitate connection, allowing us to feel the presence of those who have passed and reminding us that love endures beyond physical separation.

Dreams, too, play an important role in the healing process, often serving as a bridge to the spiritual world. Many people report encounters with their loved ones in dreams, experiencing moments of joy and closure that transcend ordinary reality. These dreams can be viewed as messages from the beyond, offering guidance, comfort, and reassurance. By paying attention to these nocturnal visitations, we can cultivate a deeper relationship with our departed loved ones, fostering a sense of continuity that enriches our lives.

Ultimately, the meaning of loss in the cycle of life is multifaceted and deeply personal. It invites us to reflect on our beliefs, engage with our emotions, and seek connections in new ways. Embracing this journey can lead to profound insights and a more compassionate understanding of both life and death. As we navigate the waters of grief, we can see strength in our shared experiences and the knowledge that love persists, guiding us on our healing path. Each step taken in remembrance not only honours those we've lost but also enriches our own journey, illuminating the beauty of existence and the enduring bonds that connect us all.

Embracing the Unknown: A Journey of Acceptance

Embracing the unknown can often feel daunting, especially in the wake of loss. As we navigate the path of grief, we are confronted with the uncertainty of what lies beyond our immediate understanding. This journey of acceptance is not just about resigning ourselves to the reality of loss; it is an invitation to explore the depths of our emotions and the mysteries of existence. By opening ourselves to the unknown, we can cultivate resilience and find peace amid turmoil, fostering a deeper connection with both our departed loved ones and our own spiritual selves.

Acceptance begins with acknowledging the myriad feelings that accompany grief. It is natural to experience a whirlwind of emotions— sadness, anger, confusion, and even moments of joy as we cherish memories of our loved ones. Embracing the unknown means allowing these feelings to coexist without judgment. This emotional openness can be transformative, serving as a bridge between our earthly experiences and the spiritual realms. By honouring our feelings, we create space for healing, enabling us to explore different facets of our grief while remaining receptive to the signs and messages from our departed.

In the context of spiritual healing and grief counselling, embracing the unknown can facilitate connections with the afterlife. Many individuals find comfort in the belief that their loved ones continue to exist in some form beyond physical death. Engaging in practices such as mediumship or spirit communication can provide reassurance and insight during this challenging time. These encounters often reveal profound messages that reaffirm the bonds of love that transcend the material world. By embracing these experiences, we can foster a greater understanding of life beyond death, enriching our journey toward acceptance.

Cultural perspectives on the afterlife also play a crucial role in how we embrace the unknown. Different cultures offer diverse rituals and ceremonies that honour the departed, allowing us to find meaning in our loss. These practices can serve as powerful tools for acceptance, guiding us through our grief while celebrating the lives of those we have lost. By participating in these traditions, we not only honour our loved ones but also create a sense of community and shared understanding, reinforcing the idea that we are not alone in our journey.

Ultimately, embracing the unknown invites philosophical reflections on life after death. This exploration may lead us to question our beliefs and confront our fears regarding mortality. Yet, it is through this inquiry that we often find solace and hope. As we think on our experiences, dreams can serve as a profound medium for connection, offering glimpses of our loved ones and insights into our healing process. By embracing the unknown, we embark on a journey of acceptance that transforms our grief into an opportunity for growth, understanding, and a deeper appreciation of the love that continues to bind us to those who have passed.

Chapter 10: Embracing the Healing Path Forward

Finding Hope during Grief

Finding hope during grief is a journey that many embark upon, often feeling lost in the depths of sorrow. It is essential to acknowledge that grief is a natural response to loss, one that can be both isolating and overwhelming. However, within this challenging process lies the potential for healing and transformation. By embracing the various dimensions of grief—spiritual, psychological, and cultural—we can begin to uncover the glimmers of hope that illuminate our path forward.

The spiritual aspects of grief offer profound avenues for connection and understanding. Many see solace in the belief that their loved ones continue to exist in some form beyond the physical realm. This perspective can be empowering, fostering a sense of ongoing relationship with those who have passed. Engaging in practices such as mediumship or spirit communication can provide comfort, allowing individuals to feel the presence of their departed loved ones. These experiences can affirm the notion that love transcends physical boundaries, igniting a spark of hope amidst the darkness of grief.

Cultural perspectives on the afterlife also play a significant role in shaping our understanding of loss. Different traditions offer unique rituals and ceremonies that honour the deceased, providing a structured way to express grief and celebrate life. These practices not only help individuals process their emotions but also connect them to a larger community that shares in their mourning. The collective experience of honouring those who have passed can foster a sense of belonging, transforming individual grief into a shared journey of remembrance and hope.

Furthermore, the psychological effects of loss and mourning can be reframed through the lens of resilience and growth. While the pain of loss can feel insurmountable, many individuals discover new strengths within themselves as they navigate their grief. The process of mourning can lead to a deeper understanding of one's values, priorities, and relationships. Embracing this transformative potential can inspire hope, as individuals learn to cherish their memories while also finding the courage to create new ones. It is a testament to the human spirit's capacity for renewal, even in the face of profound sorrow.

Lastly, dreams can serve as a powerful bridge between our worlds, offering opportunities to connect with departed loved ones. Many reports vivid dreams where they feel the presence and guidance of those they have lost, providing a sense of comfort and reassurance. These experiences can be interpreted as messages of love and support, encouraging individuals to move forward while holding their memories close. As we explore the philosophical reflections on life after death, we begin to understand that hope is not merely the absence of grief but a dynamic interplay of love, memory, and the enduring connections we share with those who have shaped our lives. In this way, hope becomes a guiding light, illuminating our healing path through the valleys of sorrow.

Tools for Ongoing Healing and Growth

In the journey of healing and growth following the loss of a loved one, it is essential to acknowledge that the process is not linear. Embracing tools that foster ongoing healing can significantly enhance our understanding of grief and allow us to navigate the complex emotional terrain. These tools can encompass a variety of practices and insights drawn from spiritual healing, psychological frameworks, and cultural rituals. Each method serves as a unique pathway to honour our departed loved ones while nurturing our own emotional well-being.

One powerful tool for ongoing healing is the practice of mindfulness and meditation. These techniques encourage individuals to remain present with their thoughts and feelings rather than suppressing or avoiding them. Through regular mindfulness practice, one can cultivate an awareness of the ebb and ow of grief, allowing them to process emotions without judgment. This can also open the door to spiritual healing, as many find that quieting the mind allows for deeper connections with their loved ones, fostering a sense of continuity and presence that transcends physical loss.

Mediumship and spirit communication offer another significant avenue for healing. Engaging with a reputable medium can provide a comforting sense of connection, facilitating conversations with those who have passed. This interaction can validate feelings of love and support, reminding us that relationships do not end with physical death. As individuals explore this realm, they may find solace in messages from their loved ones, which can inspire hope and a sense of purpose in their ongoing healing journey.

Cultural perspectives on the afterlife and the rituals associated with honouring the departed can also be instrumental in fostering ongoing growth. Different cultures have unique practices that celebrate life and death, reminding us of the universality of grief. Engaging in these rituals— whether through commemorative ceremonies, storytelling, or creating memorial spaces—can help individuals feel connected to a larger community. These practices serve to honour the memory of the deceased while simultaneously providing a supportive environment for the bereaved to express their grief and see comfort.

Lastly, dreams can serve as a profound tool for connecting with loved ones who have passed. Many people report experiencing vivid dreams that provide insight, comfort, or even messages from the departed. Keeping a dream journal can be an encouraging practice, allowing individuals to reflect on their dreams and discover the potential meanings behind them. This exploration can nurture a deeper understanding of the relationship with the deceased, validating feelings of love and connection that persist beyond death. By integrating these tools into daily life, individuals can create a rich tapestry of healing and growth, transforming their grief into a pathway toward renewed purpose and understanding.

Celebrating Life: Cherishing Memories and Moving On

Celebrating life amidst loss is a profound journey that honours the memories of those we hold dear while gently guiding us toward healing. Each memory serves as a testament to the love shared, a reminder of laughter and joy that once led our days. In this subchapter, we explore the importance of cherishing these moments, not as a means of clinging to the past but to celebrate the essence of our loved ones. By embracing their spirit through memories, we create a bridge that connects us with them, allowing their legacy to live on in our hearts.

As we navigate the complex emotions of grief, it becomes essential to cultivate practices that honour our loved ones while also facilitating our own healing. Engaging in rituals and ceremonies can provide a structured way to celebrate their lives, offering a sacred space for reflection and remembrance. These acts can range from lighting a candle in their honour to organizing a gathering of friends and family where stories are shared. Each ritual not only acknowledges the significance of our loved ones but also helps us to process our feelings, fostering a sense of community and support that is vital during the mourning period.

The Healing Path: Understanding Psychological Effects of Loss and Mourning

Cultural perspectives on the afterlife offer rich insights into how we can celebrate life in the face of death. Different cultures have unique beliefs and customs that inform their mourning practices, often emphasizing the continuity of the spirit beyond physical existence. By exploring these diverse traditions, we can find inspiration in their approaches to honouring the departed. Whether through the Day of the Dead celebrations in Mexico or the ancestral veneration practices in various Asian cultures, these rituals remind us that death is not an end but a transition, encouraging us to cherish the memories while remaining open to the possibility of continued connection.

Dreams often play a significant role in our grief journey, acting as a conduit for communication with those we have lost. Many individuals report experiencing vivid dreams where their loved ones impart wisdom, comfort, or simply a sense of presence. These encounters, whether perceived as spiritual messages or psychological manifestations, can offer solace and clarity. Embracing the possibility of these connections allows us to feel less isolated in our grief, reinforcing the belief that love transcends even the boundaries of death. By keeping a dream journal or engaging in reflective practices, one can deepen this connection and find healing in the shared memories.

Ultimately, moving on does not mean forgetting; rather, it involves integrating our memories into the tapestry of our lives. Philosophical thinking on life after death encourage us to consider what it means to truly live in the face of loss. By celebrating the lives of those we cherish, we transform our grief into gratitude, allowing their spirit to inspire us in our daily lives. This journey is not linear, but as we navigate through the layers of mourning, we can see peace in knowing that the love we shared will forever be a part of us, guiding us as we continue to honour their memory while embracing our own path forward.

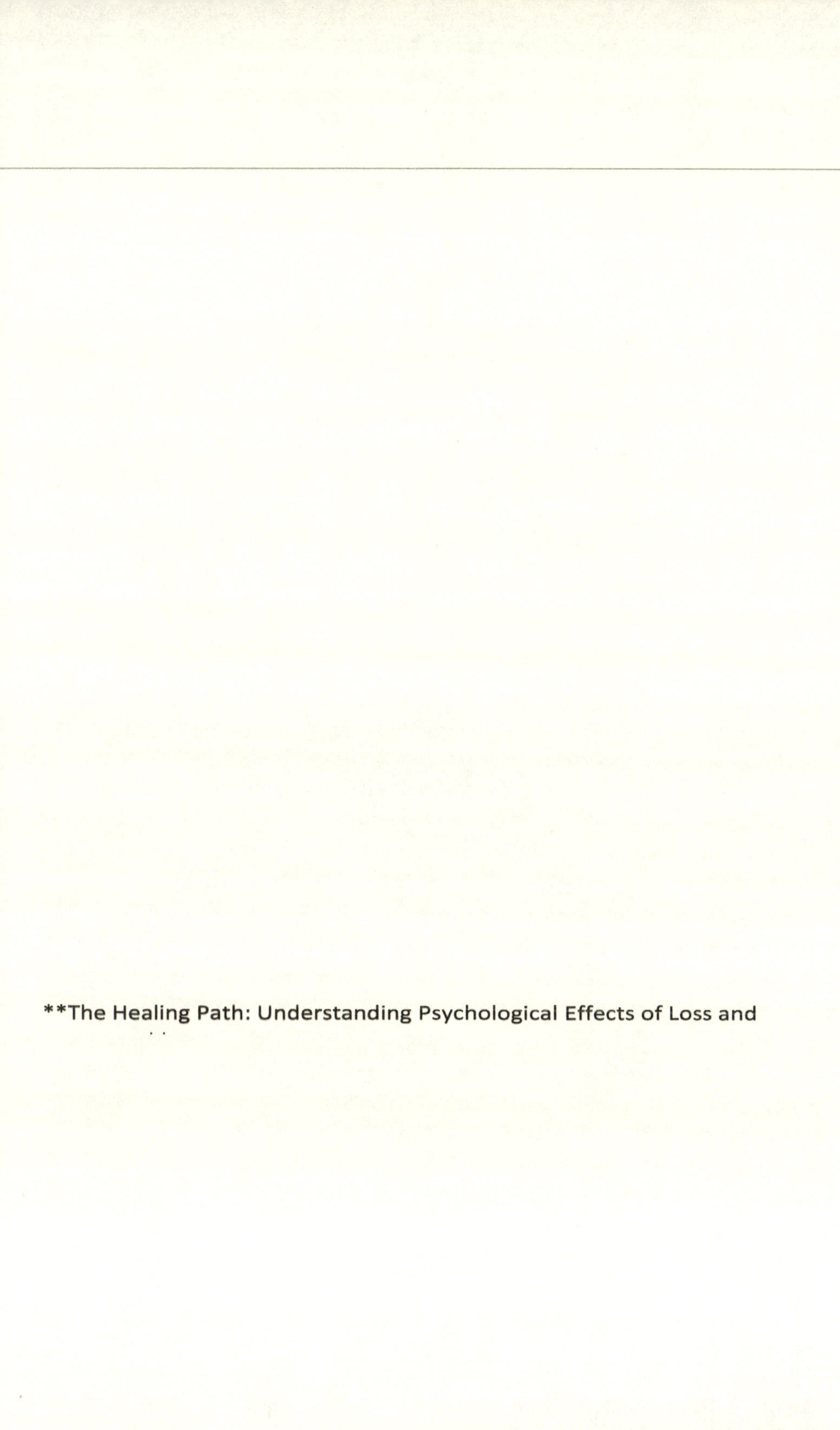

**The Healing Path: Understanding Psychological Effects of Loss and